You Only Die Once

Reflections on Mortality:
Verses from Life's Singular Journey

RITIKA

BLUEROSE PUBLISHERS
India | U.K.

Copyright © Ritika 2024

All rights reserved by author. No part of this publication may be reproduced, stored in a retrieval system or transmitted in any form or by any means, electronic, mechanical, photocopying, recording or otherwise, without the prior permission of the author. Although every precaution has been taken to verify the accuracy of the information contained herein, the publisher assume no responsibility for any errors or omissions. No liability is assumed for damages that may result from the use of information contained within.

BlueRose Publishers takes no responsibility for any damages, losses, or liabilities that may arise from the use or misuse of the information, products, or services provided in this publication.

For permissions requests or inquiries regarding this publication, please contact:

BLUEROSE PUBLISHERS
www.BlueRoseONE.com
info@bluerosepublishers.com
+91 8882 898 898
+4407342408967

ISBN: 978-93-6261-241-0

Cover design: Tahira
Typesetting: Tanya Raj Upadhyay

First Edition: August 2024

DEDICATIONS

This book is dedicated to my lovely mother who has always been the anchor of the ship in my journey of life.

ACKNOWLEDGEMENT

Someone once beautifully wrote, writing a poem is as much of a tedious but beautiful process as giving birth. This is a sentence that must be relatable to all those who have ever attempted to put their emotions into a poetry. This beautiful journey of me birthing these poems would not have been possible without the undying support of my parents. Thanks to my mother who encouraged me at every step and held me through every breakdown in this journey and thanks to my father for providing me with the correct words whenever I fell short of them. I also present my gratitude to all those who are a part of my life and those that inspired me and made me realized how every moment in life is just another film in the entire reel of the movie of our lives.

PREFACE

It was only a week till our summer breaks commenced. We had met all our teachers except our Hindi language teacher. Well, I was the kid who thought math was magic and literature was lame. Little did I know that the summer of 2016 was going to be the greatest plot twist of my life. As I was sitting in the free hindi period trying to battle the scorching Indian heat; there was a sudden uproar, " the teacher is here." I see a woman draped in a beautiful pink saree and bangs covering her forehead enter the classroom. We stand and greet her as we are programmed to. Before she even told her name she asked us what love is. This was the point I realized that literature was much more than a just a means to communicate our needs. The introductory class was about the many words we use in the Hindi language to express the different kinds of love. I was taken aback, I never knew words had such impact.

After this jaw dropping introduction to the subject, she introduced herself. Her name, Dr. Bhavana Shekhar, justified to the impact she had on me. The word "Bhavana" is a Hindi word which translates to emotions. In the first five minutes she made me feel emotions that I had not felt for years. I suddenly found myself eagerly waiting for her lessons and just like serendipity I fell in love with literature. One fine day she asked me to write a poem. I could not even frame proper sentences, how does she expect me to write a poem, I thought to myself. I gave it a shot and well it unexpectedly turned out well. That day she taught me, possibly the most important lesson of literature : words will turn out as beautifully as deeply you have felt the emotion.

A year later, she left the school but her impact on me was everlasting. I began feeling very deeply which came with its own upsides and downsides. However, the feeling of spilling my emotions on paper will always be worth any experience.

As a child, I was very imaginative and was a big movie freak. I loved watching movies multiple times and interpreting it a different way every time I watched it. On the occasion of a very huge academic slump of my life that occurred after I cracked a rat race of an examination and entered a medical college; a realization hit me: how often do we live our lives and not just suffer and drag through it. Are we actually living or just giving ourselves a benefit of doubt for a better plot twist every morning. The thought took me down the memory lane of all my bittersweet experiences. I realized how we are sold the lie of motivation, when in reality it takes far more than just that to carry ourselves through each day. This book is an attempt to romanticize different aspects of life.

I urge the readers to read each poem multiple times and I can almost be sure that each reading will leave them feeling something different from the last time.

Enjoy your reading experience!

TABLE OF CONTENTS

A BREEZY NOVEMBER 1

THE BROKEN CRIB 2

FUNERAL PYRE 3

HIDE AND SEEK 5

THE GAME OF HOMES 6

THE END OF AN ERA 7

THE BEGGAR'S REQUEST 8

MOUNT EVEREST 9

BLOOD STAIN 10

DEADLY DECEMBER 11

WHEN YOU KNOW, YOU KNOW 13

GOLD MEDAL 14

THE WORLD THROUGH NEW A NEW LENS . 15

THE ANKLET 16

TEENAGE DREAMS 18

NEW GIRL 19

THE HEMLOCK 21

A BREEZY NOVEMBER

The cold wind,

Gives a warm hug.

An unusual time to pour

life in an empty jug.

The white sheets

Now blood stained

The little woman

with her energy drained.

There is deadly silence

with the birth of chaos

Pain of life in the child's cry.

With a thousand days to live

And one to die.

THE BROKEN CRIB

Generations of bonds,

In a tiny frame

Mistakes of centuries,

A new one to blame.

A few kilos and a half.

With the new crib, they all laugh.

What a way to hide the tears,

As they teach the new one

What to fear.

The chubby face

and a happy grin.

A thousand to lose

and one to win.

Generations of bonds

Too much to weigh,

The crib is broken,

carrying it night and day.

FUNERAL PYRE

There is a desire for warmth
in everyone's heart.
I set myself on fire
And invite everyone
To feel the warmth
Never felt before.
Since none come close
to someone so cold.
All are looking for
someone to hold.
For a little hope
Is a medicine;
But too much of it
is not less of a sin.

And I hope with
the will to survive
you are not cursed.
They lay woods on me
my vision lays blurry;
for some reason unknown

no one is in a hurry.
They don't want to let go,
They like the warmth.
Now I lay in the ashes,
But they don't pour me away;
For I am cursed to
Have a Phoenix's fate.

HIDE AND SEEK

She likes to play,
All night and day.
3,2,1
The search begins.
Under the blanket she hides,
Waiting for someone
To take it off her.
Footsteps fade.
Shadows shy away.
They walk pass by,
is she that good at disguise.
She wants to be found.
She stays hidden now,
Under the bare sky.
As someone who is seen by all
But found by none.

THE GAME OF HOMES

What does it feel like, to belong?

To run somewhere after a day

That has been long.

What does it feel like

To have a roof?

That shelters you after

You have been aloof.

What does it feel

To be warm?

With people around you

To swarm.

In another life,

When time can suffice,

The answers will I find.

What's it with being a nomad?

To think of a home,

I never had!

THE END OF AN ERA

The old man gags and chokes,
Has there ever been
A poison deadlier than hope.
The cigarette of dreams,
Should one never smoke.
For the monument of
Bones and blood,
Becomes a chimney of
Burned down smiles.
Where the corpse of
A dead promise lies.
The man lies on his hospice bed,
With scars on his soul
And a lot of skin to shed.
Now still are his eyes,
Like that of a storm,
Cold is his skin
That once was warm.

THE BEGGAR'S REQUEST

An empty palm.
A chaotic calm.
The wardrobe spilled
Across the room.
Tears paint a portrait
On the walls.
The screams silence the halls.
The cold cage now warms up,
to the people
with a frozen heart.
For there is no tragedy
Greater than a forgotten art.

The street interactions
Sing the songs,
Of a legendary guest
And through the
Red, orange, green
Shout out loud
The beggar's request.

MOUNT EVEREST

How high can you go?
So much as to which
The heavens seem so low.
Oh! Petty skin and bones
What might lies in
your bricks and stones
for everything goes to dust,
if I say it is a must.
Show me your diamonds
You'll show me
Those rhinestones.
For everything I've done
You can only make clones.

Oh! So climbing the Everest
Is that your best?
Not nearly is it
the most of my quests.
For no one but me
Can move mountains,
I reside in you and
All that remains.

BLOOD STAIN

White skirts and a red stain
Slowly, staggering the walk of shame.

The soaked piece of cloth
Now, it trickles down her knees.

An excruciating pain
In her tiny body.
Their hungry, vicious eyes,
Strip her ruthlessly
A ready meal for them
She seems.

Now her eyes feel the strain
Of facing the filth of their brains.

DEADLY DECEMBER

January jesters
The February fields.
A mellow March
And the April yields
What may we expect in May
But to pray for cooler days.
In the oblivion of June.
Oh can we happily cry
drenching in the rains of July.
To lose yourself is a must,
For the tantrums of the sky,
equate my mood in August
and so the days pass
the fallen leaves, about you
they think.

But can you, when you
Planted them remember?
In a blink
You are in September
The nights are dark

But the days give away.

The fears we try and dismay.

Nothing ever lasts forever.

Nothing ever lasts forever,

Whispers in my ears

Whispers in my ears

the waning October.

The glowing ball plays hide and seek.

Welcomes a season that is

All too much.

Never a caress better

Than a breeze in November

The season of red?

Or just white snow

Covered with blood

Of those who know?

A Christmas carol?

Or the cries of the

Souls buried

Deep down the

Deadly December.

WHEN YOU KNOW, YOU KNOW

When the boat never seems to go slow,
Then all you need is a heavy blow.

Can one submit to the flow,
Or let the madness show

The stars make the dull sea glow,
But can it ever hide the dark below.

Been so low,
Even Mariana seemed shallow.

The sea of life turns into cold snow,
Because when you know, you know

GOLD MEDAL

It hangs over the nail,
The morning sun hits it
And it boasts
As not one can look at it.
Much better it is
on the nail
for it chokes my neck
I cannot carry it anymore
Even for heaven's sake.
I take it off
And now I can breathe.
Years have gone by
It is now covered with dust.

Whistling out the wind of freedom
from my mouth
I blow away,
Years of lost memories.
Only to see
What the world
saw was gold
was just mere rust.

THE WORLD THROUGH NEW A NEW LENS

I see in black and white
The deep red is just
Another shade of grey.
As comes the rainbow,
It leaves me in dismay.
I wait to cross the road.
What's the difference
Between red and green?
The zebra crossing
Full of tyre marks
is traced by my footsteps.
I cross the road

Maybe, there are colors
on the other side.
On the other side,
Lies a shop for lenses,
my only hope to witness
this world of a colorful mess.

THE ANKLET

An anklet I received,

A pleasant birthday surprise

Entangling my tiny legs

As they leap and rise

It has its own fun and jingle

As my feet, with the Earth it mingles

No more am I a little girl

I outgrew my shoes.

And my feet, they no more swirl

It has lost its shimmer

And no more glimmer.

They are now

but only shackles and chains

with all my cries that it now contains.

Each step I take towards

my grave,

these shackles, oh! my way they pave.

A year closer to my demise.

Blowing some candles, will it suffice?

With all that noise, it is hard to walk,

and I wonder if these walls could talk.

The white marble trace my blood smeared feet.

Grim Reaper, my friend, don't you cheat!

For the anklet is a lot to bear,

And I am no Hercules.

But happy here I stand on my knees.

Its cold claws dragging my feet to hell.

"Never take it off," said daddy,

And I listen to him well.

Now my world, so black and white

Is painted by the red

Pouring from my insides.

TEENAGE DREAMS

A face full of red spots

Each minute, a new thought.

A never-ending hunger

To please

Nothing to put the mind

At ease.

A cracking voice

Nothing's really a choice.

In the mind

A thousand voices scream.

Of the million unsatiated

Teenage dreams.

The sky is bleeding

through its cracks.

Dismantled are

my shelves and racks.

My hair now in

Medusa's locks.

I stare at myself

in absolute still perfection.

NEW GIRL

She likes the mountain tops

I like the beach.

I like to learn

And she loves to teach.

I keep my heart locked,

But she holds the keys.

She likes the butterflies

I love the sting of bees.

She loves the speed,

But I take it slow.

When I get too high,

She keeps me low.

I stare into her perfect eyes.

In which an ocean of

A thousand secrets lie.

Her hands, they are

cracked and dry.

Each of her scars

Hold a different cry.

A head of stone

and a heart of glass.
She spills herself
On an empty canvas.
For everyone
She might just be the new girl.
For me, she halts my world
That always swirls.

THE HEMLOCK

They say,
Eyes don't lie,
A deception I think it is
To make fools believe
in the stupid art of love;
that's what I said.
Till I met your pair
Of beautiful rhinestones.
They were sparkly,
I saw myself in them
Your lips curled up
In what I thought
Was a smile.
I remember when
you held my hand.
It felt like a tightrope
Too much for someone
so hungry for hope.

Your hug felt so warm
But I guess it was

All but a point of reference;
For a -20 and 0 holds
Much of a difference
You came for my lips
in a haste
not wanting to know
What the words
spilling out of it would taste.
Did you fall for the petals,
with no awareness of thorns?
Or maybe I was too good
At hiding.

Remember, when I told you
My house was on fire.
And saving it was
My life's desire.
I thought you gave me water
But that was just gasoline.
In the raging flames
I saw them again,
those diamonds.
As to me you turned your back.
I don't know much about

precious stones.
Or maybe I was just
Too eager to look pretty.
They say,
Eyes don't lie.

I remember you could
never read mine.
For you never desired them.
I've learnt from my mistake.
Now I don't put my eyes at stake,
for someone as stupid as me
cannot even differentiate between
A stone that is real or fake.

www.ingramcontent.com/pod-product-compliance
Lightning Source LLC
LaVergne TN
LVHW061623070526
838199LV00078B/7403